A Grown Woman's Experiences

by
Laura Taste-Sutton

PUBLICATIONS, LLC
IGNITING A FLAME FOR GOD's WORD & GOD's WISDOM

DISCLAIMER: This book contains sensitive topics that are intended for an adult audience, underage readers should receive permission from parent or guardian before reading.
He disclaimer: Whenever God, Christ or the Holy Ghost is mentioned; their pronouns are capitalized out of reverential respect.

© 2022, Laura Taste-Sutton

A GROWN WOMAN'S EXPERIENCES
Published by Wysdom Central LLC
P.O. Box 24885

Columbia, SC 29204

Cover by: danny_media
Cover's illustration: Samantha Nicole Sutton

Printed in the United States of America

All rights reserved. No part of this publication may be reproduced, stored in a retrieval system, or transmitted in any form or by any means – for example, electronic, photocopy, recording without prior written permission of the publisher. The only exception is brief quotations in printed reviews.

Although the author and publisher have made every effort to ensure that the information in this book was correct at press time, the author and publisher do not assume and hereby disclaim any liability to any party for any loss, damage or disruption caused by errors or omissions, whether such errors or omissions result from negligence, accident, or any other cause.

Scriptures taken from the Holy Bible, New International Version®, NIV®. Copyright © 1973, 1978, 1984, 2011 by Biblica, Inc.™ Used by permission of Zondervan. All rights reserved worldwide. www.zondervan.com The "NIV" and "New International Version" are trademarks registered in the United States Patent and Trademark Office by Biblica, Inc.™

Scripture taken from the KJV are taken from the KING JAMES VERSION (KJV): KING JAMES VERSION, public domain.

*"...For I know the plans I have for you", declares the Lord,
"plans to prosper you, and not harm you,
plans to give you hope and a future"
Jeremiah 29:11(NIV)*

Dedication

To Denise, Christine, Evita, and Sonya – the women that allowed me to lean on them for strength and love

To Olivia and Samantha – my babies, my girls, my heart

To Jason – Friend

To my brother Nicholas….you will always be in my heart!

Preface

I hope that these writings will help someone heal from hurtful experiences.

Writing helps externalize the pain that we feel. I now hope that this compilation of the emotions I experienced over time, will let someone know that they're not alone.

Someone understands your pain and has been where you are.

God used the love of two real friends, one sister, and one sister-in-law who loved on me through those very tough times.

I made it.

You can too.

Table of Contents

EXPERIENCES IN LIFE

Experiences 13
Mama's Blues 15
My Sista 19
Something Sweet About Thickness 23
Can These Dry Bones Live Again? 25

EXPERIENCES WITH LOVE

Big Love 31
Phat Love 33
Phat Love 2 35
Love Not Forgotten Pain Remembered 37
Unforgettable 39
I Remember Those Love Days 41
Thoughts 43
I Want 47
Hatred 49
The Decision 51
His Talk 53
Friend 57
The Storyline 59
Can These Dry Bones Live Again? II 61

EXPERIENCES WITH GOD

Don't Make No Plans for God 67
Discovery 71
From Darkness to Light 73
I Can Breathe with My Hands Raised 75
Doubt 77
Can These Dry Bones Live? III 79
Author 83

Experiences In Life

Experiences

I've laughed, I've cried
Felt insanity take over my mind.
I've been happy, been sad
Been through good, been through bad.
I've been loved, I've been hated
Felt joy, been elated
Felt cheated, felt blessed, felt nowhere in between,
But these are my experiences, oh yeah this is me.
I've been single, been married, been better, been worse
Felt trapped, then freed, felt a little off course.
I've been hurt, I've been healed
Been taught not to feel
I've been up, I've been down
Experiences are taking me to all things past
Entrenching in my soul, the only thing that lasts
Felt a lot of emotions all at the same time
Felt God with me, felt Him gone, been saved, been a sinner
Look inside and see my inner
Experiences………

Reflections from the Author:

I encourage you to draw strength from the knowledge that God knows the direction you are going in. The hills and valleys may be hard to travel through, but the end of your journey will be so much richer when you look back and see how far you traveled. We say it often, but it's true- Trust the process.

Jeremiah 29:11 NIV
"For I know the plans I have for you," declares the LORD, "plans to prosper you and not to harm you, plans to give you hope and a future."

What is your vision for yourself?

_____
_____
_____
_____
_____
_____
_____
_____
_____

Mama's Blues

I feel like such a failure as a mother sometimes
It's like me and my daughter are never speaking the same rhyme.

I push, she pulls, and we create such negative tension
Hard stresses that she puts me through are beyond my comprehension.

I get so angry and even sad when this child does not listen
Trying to save her from the hard knocks that I've already been in.

I'm trying to make her better than me, greater than me, a woman of power
She refuses to hear when I speak softly but gets angry when I speak louder.

She gets mad and indigent, and uses sarcastic phrases
Make me want to get a switch and beat her out of these teenage phases.

I got the mama blues in my heart real strong
The kind that wants to kick her out even though I feel it's wrong.

Mama's Blues

She's just like ungrateful folks who refuse to listen to just good reason
They reject you, resent you, and take your love for their own selfish treason!

I got the mama blues heart so heavy, I cannot even speak
I feel like giving up, stop trying, and let her roll down fool's creek.

I see struggle in her future, and pain in her days
If she doesn't change her hard-headed, teenage ways.

Not saying I'm perfect, or even that I'm better than
But I use a lot more common sense in my well thought out plans.

Maybe as her mama, I don't always understand what she's going through
Failing to reckon when she screams in anger "Mama, I'm not like you!"

I keep praying that God gives me strength every day
To help me through these mama blues, and love this child anyway.

Despite her disrespect, ungratefulness, and the "I know it all" attitude
I'll take a deep breath, count to ten, and reset my fortitude.

My heart is so full; brimming with love, cause this child is who I birthed
And I'm determined to do all I can, to teach my girl how much she's worth.

In the meantime, it will take all my might and faith in God to do what I have to do
To overcome this battle and win the fight against this unrelenting Mama's Blues!

Reflections from the Author:

Although the journey raising my youngest daughter was a challenge, I 've learned so much about her, and so much about myself. My daughter took many liberties in telling me when I was wrong, but once we established the proper and respectful ways to verbalize her grievances and opinions, I promised her and myself that I would listen and try to see her point of view. It's been a rewarding experience for both of us.

Proverbs 22:6 KJV
Train up a child in the way he should go: And when he is old he will not depart from it.

Do you need to make a better connection with your child? What can you do to listen more?

_____

_____

_____

_____

_____

_____

_____

My Sista

One day
You took my family to a movie
Paid for us
Treated my kids to popcorn
Told a joke and made me laugh
You walked us to our car
You secretly put $50 in my hand
Those simple acts were a reminder that
God had not forgotten me
Thanks to my Sista.

Then
I was turning 50
Sadness settled over me divorced
Getting older, alone single mother
It seemed God was gone again
You called
I said no to my birthday
Nothing to celebrate
You insisted and we did it
I was grateful
For my Sista.

Then
I had a little meltdown
You drove from two hours away
Spent time with me
Took me out to dinner and laughed with my kids
My heart was lifted for a moment
I felt God again
Because of my Sista.

Then
Looking at me, everything seems fine
No one at work knew
That I was a horrible person
Why else would I be deserted?
And have deserted kids
I put on the best act
But you knew
Stopped by my office and hugged me
Told me you loved me
I didn't feel loved
But by you my Sista.

Then
I called you crying
Memories had my heart dying
You read a bible scripture
It was like a healing balm
I felt better
I told you I was grateful
You reminded me that I was a woman

My Sista

A strong, powerful woman
Then I got your text
A message of strength
That came from you my Sista.

Then
I was in church one Sunday
Plastered a smile on my face
Pain in my heart
I had to stay strong, had to go on
I was clapping my hands
Then raising my hands
Then tears falling, my heart breaking
I felt a hand on my right shoulder
And one on my left
It was you, my daughters
Loving me like my Sistas.

Dedicated to:
Denise, Christine, Sonya, Evita, Olivia & Samantha

Something Sweet About Thickness

All my youth, I've been big. My thighs, butt, and breasts.
I grew up feeling self-conscious about why I didn't look like the rest
Of the girls, thin and curvy, seemed God gave it to them, right?
In all the places, I wanted less of, a body a brotha' called tight!

I imagined myself with a small waist, and well-rounded hips
36 C cups, long legs, high cheeks, and kissable lips.
Many times, ugly thoughts overtook me; made me sad, and depressed.
Disgusted at myself and believed myself less.

But now, as a woman with wisdom and added age,
I outgrew the self-hatred and moved past that stage
And became self-aware that there's beauty in me,
Created with, composed of, saturated distinctively.

A revelation, appreciation, something sweet about thickness.
My ancestry, my heritage, the DNA of my blackness.
Big-boned, heavy girl is what they use to call me.
Never referred to as passionate, beautiful, or hot, and sexy.

Something Sweet About Thickness

In case you didn't know, there's something sweet about thickness,
Just fall into my stuff, my folds, my layers, get lost in all its richness!
Everywhere you touch and explore, there's soft fullness to grab hold.
From supple big breasts to warm thick thighs, wonders to behold!

I'm a woman that can be, can do, and not let slim curves dictate my station.
No longer let derogatory opinions make less of God's creation.
See… I now believe God gave me a measure that was always handed right
Because I'm head-to-toe delicious at least to me, and more in God's sight!

Oh yeah! There's something sweet about thickness,
Destroying a girl's self-esteem, you got my forgiveness.
Nothing is more powerful than God setting the record straight.
What He designed is always perfect; shame, you think it's only about weight.

I'm a special, complex, interpersonal delight of why the "wo-man"
Fits jointly, securely, perfectly…."the verb" of any man.
So girl, put your high heels on, strut your stuff, put the critics to shame.
My name's Sweet Thickness, call me Black Bigness, ain't no shame in my game!

Can These Dry Bones Live Again?

Dry and crumbled, no life within.
No marrow, just sorrow no happiness to begin.
These bones of our love seem long past dead.
We wallow in dust, just tears to shed.
Dry bones can you speak?
Is it life that you seek?
Dry bones can you live?
The life only God can give.
Seeking to restore
What we had before.
Thinking it's the end
We're no longer friends.
So, I ask this question of you;
 No one else to answer true.
Can these dry bones live?
This life that only God can give.
Bones that are without substance to surround.
Bones of frail love lay wasted on the ground.
Can these dry bones live Lord, only You know?!

Can These Dry Bones Live Again?

"Speak to them," God said, so its life will flow.
With our faith and the power of God's word,
Restoration of our hearts because we heard
The power of its truth we now have gained
And renewed our love, dry bones you can live again.

Reflections from the Author:

I felt my life was over - literally dry, dead bones, during the years of my heartbreak! My faith and (I felt) my life were buried in the driest desert with no hope of living again. Sometimes, what we go through makes us feel that way. Oh, but I thank God that he can breathe life back into our circumstances. Make our life rise up, and live again by healing our heart, renewing our hope, and strengthening our mind. Won't he do it!

Experiences With Love

Big Love

I did my nails today, French manicured pearly white
Got my hair done too, French twist, pin curls done up just right.
Got my toes done, hot pink, sexy with a wild design
New dress, new shoes, I've gotta make myself really fine.
Bought a real rose you know, to pin up in my hair
My face all colored pretty, hoping he would stare
At me
So he'll see
How much I can be
A woman
For a man
To love just as much
Prove to be tender with a gentle touch.
A virtuous woman, meet all his needs in many ways to discover
Take him places, get in new spaces, he'll need days to recover.
Cause overlooking me cause I'm big would certainly be real tragic
Cause I'm strong, and fearless, and creative, for me is a natural habit.
I got all dressed up looking beautiful to show you all I can be
Greatness, intelligence, and faithfulness all wrapped up in me.

Big Love

I got love, BIG love that I can share
Give you all of me; you'll see, just meet me there.
It's not my size I tell you that's worth speaking of
But it's my heart even greater still, filled with that big, big love!

Phat Love

There's a guy in my class that sits in front of me - row three.
I stare at him often of course, but he never looks back at me.
I notice everything about him; his eyes, his smile, his hair
To think he would notice me, to dream of it, I wouldn't dare!

He sits in class and observes most of the time.
Wonder if he knows I'm digging him, if he knows I think he's fine.
He's cool with his classroom answers, admits when he is wrong
He just nods and smiles, that sexy smile. I can love on him all day long!

Been in the back of his class almost all this school year,
Daydreaming and wishing, but hopelessly living in fear.
Afraid a man so fine would never see me,
As big as I am, to one like him I don't exist, I could never be.

He probably prefers the big breasts, small waist and big hip girls, hitting all three.
He probably doesn't want any thick girl, phat girl, a pool of self-hate misery.

Phat Love

Guess I'll stay in the back of the class and fantasize about this dream.
Cause that's the closest I'll ever get, of this phat girl being seen.

Wish I could be his girl all wrapped up in his smile,
bathed in his love, settled in his arms, and have him talk to me for a while.
Wonder what he would say, how would his sweet words flow
With the tune of his music, the skip of his vibe, I wonder how it would go.

The bell rings, and he stands to leave, I know my reverie is over.
I blink and awaken to realize he is far from being my lover.
Instead of walking away, he pauses, turns, and looks in my direction.
How can a man be so fine? Only God can make such perfection!

He's in front of me now, my heart is racing, I need to run and hide.
God, I'm not ready, I need more work on my debilitating foolish pride.
He grabs my hand to deliver a touch like sun ray's fire-scorched.
And whispered words I thought never to hear, his purpose to exhort.

"You're beautiful." The softest words brushed gently across my ear. Broke down the prison stronghold of days of my self-conscious fear.
Cause he's now not just a guy in class that sits in front of me.
For tomorrow, I can sneak a peek as he looks back and smiles at me.

Phat Love 2

There's a girl in my class that sits behind me - three rows back.
Her averted eyes when I enter the room, speaks self-confidence is what she lacks.
I walk in smooth and take my seat trying to throw a smile her way.
I notice everything about her lips, her hair, and the curve of her hips when she walks away.

She sits in class and stays quiet most of the time.
Wonder if she knows I'm digging her, if she knows I think she's fine.
She must think I don't see her, but I do, yet to approach her I wouldn't dare!
I want to look back, see her pretty face, all day long just to stare.

So, I play it cool with my classroom answers, admit when I'm wrong.
I just nod my head, and smile really sexy, as I think about loving on her all day long!
She's been in the back of my class almost all this school year.
I've been daydreaming and wishing I could talk to her, without this ego fear.

Of being rejected by a natural beauty afraid she would never see me
Cause I like big breasts, big hips, a pretty face - that girl hitting all three.

Wishing she could be my girl wrapped in her blossom soft smile, bathed in her love, settled in her arms, and have her talk to me for a while.

Wonder what she would say, how her sweet words would flow
The tune of her music, the skip of her vibe, I wonder how it would go.
The bell rings, I stand to leave, I know my reverie is over,
I blink and awaken to realize she is far from being my lover.

Instead of walking away, I pause, turn, and look in her direction.
How can a woman be so fine? Only God can make such perfection!
She's in front of me now, but seems to want to run and hide.
God, I'm not ready, I need more work on my debilitating foolish pride.

I grab her hand and feel her touch like sun ray's fire-scorched
And whispered words I thought I would never say, my purpose to exhort
"You're beautiful." The softest words brushed gently across her ear. Broke down the prison stronghold of days of her self-conscious fear.

Cause she's now, not just a girl in class that sits in the back of me
For tomorrow, I can sneak a peek back at her as she smiles and looks at me.

Love Not Forgotten Pain Remembered

Love not forgotten like the first hint of light that the sun brings to the day

Love like the way my body tingles from touches you use to give in that sensual, sexy way.

I can't forget Love, yet it's been some years

Love that made me happy some days, while others it brought me tears.

Should I, could I, still be in love with you

After everything you and I failed to do.

I still have regrets that the Love is gone

We both fought some battles that nobody won!

You're there, I'm here, the space between us reminds me of the pain

Love may not be forgotten, and yet the heartbreak remains.

We laughed many days and shared intimate times

But my empty arms and painful heart cannot be denied.

That my Love for you is not forgotten, but the ache remembers clear

You stopped loving me, wanting me, and didn't need me to be near.

I wish now that we would have spoken more words our hearts needed to say

It may have dissipated the darkened cloud that covered our sunlit life so grey.

Still, I can't forget Love, I didn't know how much until pain took its place

Love not forgotten; this heartbreak pain will take God's healing balm of Grace.

Unforgettable

There was a special friend that I knew a few years ago
One of my inspirations that pushed me to my higher plateau
To go beyond this moment of myself and reach for a better me
To be unpredictable, and un-conforming as the waves of the gallant sea

A friend that was a brother whose heart seemed joined to mine Who understood my pain, sorrows and struggles all combined Suffering alone when I'm happy it's only me "Unforgettable", cannot be replaced in me except distantly

Head hung low; tears streak my cheeks so I cannot smile
Except when I can spend some time with him in a dream for just a while
While we're there, I tell how I miss what was, what is "Unforgettable"
And he reminds me I'm God's design he knew as his "Incredible".

Brother of my spirit so close a reflection of me
Oh I wish this dream could last; I see you so seldomly
I want you back, I need you here
To hold my hand and calm my fears
But a dream is just a dream much fainter than a wish
What's left is appreciation of a brother I once called Nicholas.

I Remember Those Love Days

Love felt so good back in those simple days
I had thoughts of me getting with you in so many love ways
We were crazy in love when
Love was new then
And we believed in all our oneness
Oh, I remember I was fascinated by those warm, brown eyes
And you loved the way my hips sort of rise
When I walked and swayed just to tease you and please you
Cause I was your slave, you were my king
Secluded in our new love so easily forgot about the world outside
Cause we were in love and making love, and sharing love
There were no disguises
There were no surprises

I Remember Those Love Days

About who I was, or who you were,
We lay with naked hearts and naked bodies
In our first place, with just enough space for love to grow in ways that transformed us
Yeah, I remember those days when
Loving you was easy, and sweet
We were pure from the disease of routine
Think back, you know what I mean
I rubbed on you, you loved on me
And there was forever in between.
Image of you in my eyes like Aegean stars
A hope of long lasting love upon you for which I gaze
And in your heart the beat of my rhythm constant you will find
As long as we remember those simple love days.

Thoughts

For the past several days, Thoughts had roamed and intermittently began to stray.
Suddenly about my husband whom I had not thought about in days.
I was confused about these Thoughts of him so firm was my resolve
To settle down and accept my choice of loneliness; to watch my life evolve.

It was months ago we parted, a rift that had come between.
Hurt, pain, and emptiness now live where once our love was clearly seen.
Hollow cisterns empty of substance, dry dust settled all around.
All our hopes, our dreams, and passions lay futilely crumbled on the ground.

Thoughts of anguish from imprisonment laid siege upon my mind.
Joy arrested, peace restrained and sorrow captured time.
But at his exodus, my spirit quieted, my soul had now ceased to rage.
So end the years of torrent storms between, that used to haunt at every stage.

Thoughts

I thought it done, life's tale now anew with just a single strand, I once had loved and now have lost, uncertain if I will begin again. Then suddenly Thoughts began to invade this quiet place within. It crept upon me unawares still not sure just how Thoughts got in.

Maybe I'd been thinking how far down this road we'll travel. A bended road that winds and turns with doubt the layered gravel. Stirred Thoughts of the love lost to come upon me and demand an audience.
But I forebode the deserted place and invited Thoughts in just this once.

We talked a while and sometimes argued, about who was right or wrong
Thoughts would make me feel like on me the guilt of my love lost belonged
My heart would hurt and my mind would strain as I tried to push Thoughts out.
Trying to regain coveted peace of time without Thoughts and with no doubt.

Alas, still confused about these Thoughts of him so firm was my resolve.
To settle down again, accept my choice of loneliness, and watch my life evolve.

Reflections from the Author:

I had to make this scripture a part of my daily life. Read it, sleep with it on my mind. and wake up thinking about how it's all going to work out even though it didn't look like it, and it sure didn't feel like it! Every time I ran into a proverbial wall or felt defeated by something that went wrong, I quoted this scripture to remind myself - It's going to be ok.

Romans 8:28 NIV
And we know that in all things God works for the good of those who love him, who have been called according to his purpose.

What are the proverbial walls or unaccomplished goals you need faith to conquer and overcome?

_____

_____

_____

_____

_____

_____

_____

I Want

I want to feel the softness of love circle around my heart
I want to know the pain and sorrow engulf me cause from my love, I am apart
I want to know how strong his hold, how strong his arms around me take
I want to know of passion, soft, hard when love to me he makes
I want to know of feeling our friendship, together or alone
I want laughter, joy, sadness, and crying even away from me or home
I want to know the peace of trust and less the cruelty of deceit
I want to know forgiveness, reconciled, we find at each other's feet
I want to know the power of prayer, as we lean upon our faith
I want to know how oneness of spirit, destroys the evil against our inherent fate
I want to know how this today, or tomorrow will bring about new things
I want to know the hope of Jesus that elevates us to ride upon His wings
I want to walk the sun-drenched days with you
I want to spend the cool blue nights there too
I want in your arms, in your bosom as much as time will give
I want to die in love with you, as long as we shall live.
I just want you!

Hatred

Husbands do you hate yourselves that much?
And look at yourself in self-disgust?
Do you abhor the sight of the mirror?
Ugliness and horror ever drawing nearer.
I have never seen such hatred towards one's own self as you
Starved of love, deprived of needs
Worthless is what you'll always believe
You allow the darkness to surround you
Fear has overtaken
Unhappiness has been your friend; your heart is always aching
What peace do you know? What joy is yours?
How can you reconcile?
Fill the emptiness of your hurt and bring comfort for a while
Love her now as you love yourself, make that self-sacrifice
Christ loved the Church to destroy the hate the day He gave His life!
Now stand up and be the king that for so long she has waited
Let agape love be your strength and break the bonds of pride's self-hatred!

The Decision

Over two months, we have been at odds
Not speaking
Only seeking
How to sustain the silence
I have been angry the whole time
That our love is dead
Every night in bed
I pray, I cry because our souls are so far apart
I feel empty space inside because love left me long ago
Just want to be free
From feeling empty
And have the pulse of my heart reflect life again
It's so hard in this relationship not knowing where you stand
Should I go or stay
Either way, make the pain go away
If only I knew how to fix us- who are so badly broken
Every time I think about trying us again
Fear tightly grips
My mind starts to trip
I get overwhelmed with unhappiness and uncertainty that we will never work!
When I think about the decision, I cry

The Decision

I wonder why
I should continue to abide
In this sea of sorrow of unfulfilled love, drowning, afraid, given up
But then, we spoke our feelings a moment for one night
We both expressed
Now we have less
Things we must discuss to find our way out of this mess
Despite all this emotional trauma between us
I want to make love with you
I think you want to be with me too
We have been strangers for so long, just not sure
how to connect anymore
Just not sure of "The Decision".

His Talk

She got all of my control and she will not let it go
Stopping a brotha from working his hustle
Interrupting my flow.
Trying to do my thing whatever it is
Want to do it my way
But she dumps on me, deflating my mojo fizz.
I get mad sometimes; tell her to stay out of my space
Working on making my super fly
Practicing my mac, my style, want to walk with my kind of grace.
I don't think I'm big time…I just know I am
Need her to give me my props
Respect, accept, stand by me, like "I'm the man."
Ok so, I don't finish everything I start, come up with ideas that dive
But I'm a mover, a shaker, ya know
So what if it fails? at least I tried.
I feel like I'm in her shadow, not the one in control
Want to be who I'm supposed to be
Want her to need me, love me from the bottom of her soul,
Look at her standing there with my manhood in her hand
Juggling my maleness like a circus act
Dissing a brotha like only a black woman can.
Tired of coming with my hat in my hand, begging on my knee

His Talk

I got my ego to think of
She always makes me feel less than who I want to be.
Yeah, I give her a hard time and ignore her sometimes too
Under the circumstances can you blame a brotha
For doing what he do.
Trust me, I can stand on my own two feet
Don't always need her checking me
I want to say, "I got this baby!" I wish that she could see.
That I'm a man in God's own image, strong and fearlessly true
This is real talk, I recognize my imperfections
We both got plenty of faults, but that ain't nothing new.
So no more feeling like I'm in her shadow, taking back my control
 I stepped to her and embraced her like I was supposed to do
She smiled, and kissed me with sweet love from the bottom
of her soul.

Reflections from the Author:

A relationship is one of the most complex things to maneuver, however God intended it to be one of the most simplistic. The message is pretty straightforward, however, marriages go through so many obstacles and challenges. There are scriptural instructions for wives as well. Right now, I want women to know that God wants you to be loved, cared for, and treasured like He does for His church!

Ephesians 5:25 KJV
Husbands, love your wives, even as Christ also loved the church, and gave himself for it.

What are the things you want to work on together with your partner?

_____

_____

_____

_____

_____

_____

_____

_____

Friend

I don't think it's a good idea that we go back to the way we were
Getting back together after all this time; I don't think it should occur.

We've had so many tough times; many more bad times than we had good
What I said as a man, and what you felt as my wife, so many things we misunderstood.

Eighteen years of time we shared determined to build a life I promised to be your husband and you promised to be my wife.

But now as a man, I have mistakes to fix, self-love to find, and for sins, I must repay
I can admit that to your face my dear, cause your forgiveness made the way.

A virtuous woman you proved to be, worthy of my respect and praise
I should not have taken you for granted and loved you with all my ways.

Friend

As a man, I take the blame for my part that caused us this wretched pain
Maybe I'm not good at love, it's just not me, a second chance I have not gained.

Who I was back then, took a long, long road swept with dry and sanded dust
My heart now hardened by single life's confinement; myself I find hard to trust.

My hands are rough, my eyes now dim, although lessons I have learned
Self-exile from love's sweetest beauty, I feel is what I've earned.

But will always remember the day, I asked your fair love when standing upon that stage
Promising to be your man, your cover, with a ring you to me engaged.

I think about you even now, a connection that may never end
Knowing I may never call you wife again, but at least I can call you – friend!

The Storyline

How do I begin this thing?
In the middle, the start, or at the end?
Of how hard it's been over the years
So many tears, ever-growing fears.

Of what I couldn't control, didn't understand and couldn't see
What Love was trying to do in me, for me, with me, to me!
Many days of you pulling me, me pulling you
Directions don't know where to go or what to do……

I loved you so much a time ago
Everything else in my life, I easily let go
So I could start a new story, called "Once upon a time… with you
Thought together there was nothing we couldn't do.

The storyline has changed from fairy tale to reality
You were no longer you and I was no longer me
Our hurt took away the sweetness and the propensity to care
Treated me like I didn't matter, and that you were not there.

The Storyline

We didn't talk things through and to get each side of the storyline
Can't say that now, cause things have changed with time
So many things gone bad, so many things have gone amiss
We've lost our way, gotten off track, not even sure we can pray about this.

We are broken, missing pieces, shattered hearts and hollow hands
You go one way, I go that, in different places now we stand
What's my story, do you even want to know
Do you even care to know how this thing goes
This thing we call our storyline.

Can These Dry Bones Live Again? II

When I looked out across the dry sand of my life
And see the highs and the lows of what the wind created That which has taken the substance of our "we" now lay scattered and deflated
The dryness of our bones so brittle and cracked beyond repair
A breath of dust caught in the wind just a whisper in the air
The struggles over who I was, and who you were proved hard to overcome
Putting pieces back together from this our broken life would be ok for some
Flesh dissolved, marrow crusted, all the sinews disjointed
For us the brittle bones of our lives
are too fragile
Nothing agile
Void of life
No longer your wife
You swore to protect, love, honor, and cherish me
Be the strength and the substance to always feed me
But instead, you cheated, dishonored, and embellished me
With lies and deceit in your heart, you shamed me

Can these dry bones live again?
Lord, You know
How the story goes
It will take Your breath, Your power, Your Spirit
To recreate us and put life back in this love, these lives, your man,
his wife, his soul, her spirit, our lives, no strife
"I'm sorry", "forgive me", "I love you" for you I'm feeling
Like the balm of Gilead; these words send true healing
Can these dry bones live?
Lord, You know!

Reflections from the Author:

Ezekiel 37:1-10 NIV
Then he said to me, "Prophesy to these bones and say to them, 'Dry bones, hear the word of the Lord! This is what the Sovereign Lord says to these bones: I will make breath enter you, and you will come to life.

What part of your life do you need life breathed back into?

_____

_____

_____

_____

_____

_____

_____

_____

_____

_____

_____

Experiences with God

Don't Make No Plans for God

Be careful what you pray for when you ask
"Lord, please do it."

You just might get what you want, a different design than you had in mind
But it's done all before you knew it.

See, God ain't no once a year Santa Claus, or some genie in a bottle
Can't just snap your fingers, mutter some words, and just simply expect Him to follow.

God does things His way, or no way, taking all things into account
He measures your heart, your worth, your courage
I know you had your thoughts on how the role should play.
See, He knows what you're all about....

You wanted it done today not tomorrow, you wanted to buy not borrow.
Change direction from the hard choices; wanted to leave, not stay.

But you missed that part when he said, "My ways are not yours…"
I make, I destroy, I open, and close your doors.

Don't Make No Plans for God

He knows when you get up, sit down, go out and come in,
When you walk, when you run around confusion block and back again.

So, don't make no plans for God, He works on His own timetable. History has already confirmed, and you know for yourself that God is able!

So don't set no date, don't schedule no time…although waiting is very hard
He will do, what He do, when He do, so don't make no plans for God.

Reflections from the Author:

Wow, imagine that the God of the universe has made plans for all of his creation including YOU! How special you are that he took time to design the life befitting a queen.

Psalm 33:11 NIV
But the plans of the LORD stand firm forever, the purposes of his heart through all generations.

What are some of your goals and plans?

_____

_____

_____

_____

_____

Discovery

There was a part of me that I'm just finding out.
It was hidden, concealed, and overshadowed with doubt.
A side crushed from the pain, and burdens I carried.
Didn't know I was bruised, sadness that tarried.

But a man who knew how to love saw me while I was there.
In spite of the darkness, His love saw my despair.
He drew closer, nearer, drawn by my heart.
He felt its flutter, though lost in the dark.

One night, I was desperate, awakened in fear.
Felt cold chills, I didn't know He was near.
Till He touched me, love engulfed me, like a sun setting for the day.
Didn't know that a man could love me that way.

In Him, I discovered that I was a beauty; worthwhile, a treasure.
One He thought to die for; against His life, He thought to measure.
I discovered I am beloved; not by man or even self shall I compare.
I discovered I am light; under darkness no longer hidden there.

Discovery

The piece of me that was lost because of hurt, sin, and shame.
I found, renewed, alive because His voice called my name.
No more sadness, nor darkness, a vessel empty and dry.
Love found me, Jesus loved me, I discovered was the only reason why!

From Darkness to Light

Dim and dark are the eyes of me
Less of two I cannot see
Darkness surrounding me seem everyday
Hinders the who in me, I've lost my way
I search and seek for light to know
To start my journey one day I'll go
A veil that covers, a blanket that hides
Nowhere shall light in me resides
But then a whisper so softly speaks
Like a breeze that travels lightly across my cheeks
Tells me kindly from darkness rise
Rekindle light within my eyes
Reminds me that all things I can do
The spirit of hope takes me back to where I once knew
For no shadows of failure shall hold me tight
As Love's power leads me from darkness to light

I Can Breathe with My Hands Raised

I laid in the corner, knees to my chin, curled in a human ball
Crushed as close as I could get against the bathroom wall
Tears stung my eyes and stained my cheeks
Fear gripping, loneliness hovering, sadness surrounding me for weeks.

I could hear many voices shouting false truths in my clouded mind
Accusing me of past mistakes to prove failure in my future was all I'd ever find
A moan of pity and wringing hands added to my distress
I felt attacked and almost defeated and completely under duress.

I felt weak and struggled to simply find answers that would guide me
To ease my troubled mind
I reached and stretched my hands up in the air
Grasping and clutching battered hope to believe someone to be there.

I Can Breathe with My Hands Raised

I felt the tension in my chest, the erratic beating of my pulse so wild
As the snickering of the hurtful truths showed me as a sinful child.

I couldn't breathe, for fear of being lost had taken my breath away,
I was choking on all the madness, barely hearing the tiniest voice say
Forgiveness, redemption, salvation, My sacrifice has made the way
With hope of hope, I pushed again to reach beyond the break.

Doubt

How weak and insecure you are
With your pettiness of fear and doubt
Especially when you profess to know God
Stand up girl and cast that thing out!
I'm ashamed of how you quiver and cower
Because the "I" in you decrees I'm not sure, I don't know
 Well, get over it on your knees!
Don't tell me you're afraid of the "un" in uncertainty
Allowing doubt to grip your mind
Refuse to accept the false you see
Don't be fooled again this time
Be the conqueror I know you are
A measure of faith is what you got
Your future and your "can-do" aligned
A doubtful Sarah is what you're not
So, let's make it happen for you my sister
With "I can", "I will", "I do"
And remember by faith, your God is with ya
To way beyond this day you accept your gospel truth!

Can These Dry Bones Live?
III

I'm not asking if dry bones can live this time
Because these bones have risen and I'm feeling just fine
The joints repaired from being cracked and broken
The sinews renewed filled with joy outspoken
I am no longer just a breath of dust caught in the wind.

I feel the restoration of agape love filling my soul again
Lord, You promised to protect, love, and keep me
Been the strength and the substance that has set me free
You cherished me, honored me and loved me exponentially
With truth, and honesty by Your grace You've strengthened me.

Can these dry bones live again?
Lord, you know
How the story goes
It will take Your GRACE, Your breath, Your power, Your Spirit
To recreate the formation, and put life back in it.

Can These Dry Bones Live? III

Can these dry bones live again?
Lord, only You know
The truth, dry cracked bones can be raised
pushed through the bowels of the earth to reach sun-drenched rays.

Not by might, nor power, but by the breath of GRACE
that removes the decay from my life and sanctifies my space
Within my heart, my mind GRACE placates my soul
and lifts me, sustains me, and makes me whole.

See GRACE is the sinew that surrounds these dry bones
 it's the life's blood that runs through the veins of my own Self-
love, self-image, a replication of the only One
That gives me strength to say, "Dry bones - I'm done!"

A GROWN WOMAN'S EXPERIENCES
NOTES FOR YOU BY YOU

Author
Laura Taste-Sutton

Available for Speaking Engagements & Poetry Events
Email: thesuttonprofessional@gmail.com

www.ingramcontent.com/pod-product-compliance
Lightning Source LLC
LaVergne TN
LVHW051527070426
835507LV00023B/3357